AF483662

First hardcover edition — August 2022

ISBN 979-8-2180-1767-5 (hardcover)

Marty the Matzah Loses His Butt

A Passover story

Written and illustrated by Joel Lewenstein

To Gideon, for laughing at enough of my butt jokes
to make me think I could write a book of them.

To Nicole, for the exact same thing.

•

And to Simon, for taking long naps so I could draw.

Marty the Matzah awoke with a grin,
Knowing that Passover was soon to begin.

He climbed out of his box, yelled "Hip hip hooray!"
Then started preparing for his most special day.

On Pesach his family didn't eat bread
But rather made meals using matzah instead.

No bagels, no pasta, no baking with leaven.
This week Marty was truly in heaven.

Some people got bored eating matzah so long,
But this year Marty would prove them all wrong.

"Just a stale cracker?! Oh no, not I!"
"Try me as matzah pizza or matzah brei"

Passover began with the big seder meal.
Marty welcomed his friends with vigor and zeal.

"Hiya Parse!" He chirped to the delightful green herb.
Fresh and springlike, her leaves were superb.
"Enjoy staying dry," she said jealously.
"While I'm dunked in water that's cold and salty!"

"L'chaim!" He bellowed to the glasses of wine,
Whose sparkling crystal looked just divine.
"We can't stay to talk, try as we might,"
"They'll drink and refill us four times tonight!"

Out on a cane hobbled wisened Maror,
An old bitter herb who'd seen all this before.

"Hey Gramps!" Marty yelled to his one good ear.
Maror sighed: "My boy, you do this each year,"
"I'm so glad to see you're excited for seder,"
"But just remember what happens to you later..."

But Marty ignored him — what did he know?
Soon came Matzah Time, he starred in this show.

Speaking of starring, it was time to think through
What he'd perform for this year's debut.

He wanted to show off his versatility.
Perhaps a tap dance? Juggling? A concerto, or three?

Then it was time, he heard his name called.
The family was staring at him, enthralled.

Dad picked him up, said the matzah prayer.
Marty's excitement was too much to bear.

He swelled up proudly, ready to strut,
But then heard a CRACK and....

Off.

Came.

His.

Butt!

"My tuchus!" He thought, "Oy vey is this bad."
As he shot a betrayed look upwards at Dad.

"Hey Pops, where do you think you're goin'?"
But Dad left the room to hide the afikomen.

"Hide!?" Thought Marty, glaring at the old man.
This week was not starting according to plan.

He'd dreamed of being in soup, or matzah PB&J,
At least covered in chocolate and eaten that way.

But all hopes were dashed by Dad's daring ambush,
So he began plotting ways to recover his tush.

The family, oblivious, continued the seder,
But Marty wanted his heinie back sooner than later.

Marty heard a small boy asking four questions
And noticed his fanny got zero mentions.

Marty inched over and hissed in his ear:
"Would you mind asking after my keister, my dear?"

Next came the story of Jews and Pharaoh
And how out of Egypt they wanted to go.

When Pharoah refused, God sent plagues like a curse:
Frogs, hail, and darkness, and some that were worse.

Marty, unimpressed: "Just frogs that could jump?"
"How'd Pharoah like to be missing his rump?!"

The family ate. Marty's hopes started to dim.
The prospects of reunion were looking quite grim.

He cried: "Passover sure is a dismal affair,
I guess I'll say bye to my sweet derrière."

The kid at the table heard Marty's cries,
Cleared his throat loudly, and rolled his brown eyes.

"Just give us a minute, you unleavened snack!
"After dinner we'll find it and give it right back."

Plates were cleared. Marty yelled: "I don't mean to be blunt,"
"But seems high time for an afikomen hunt!"

The kids ran out to search, with big whoops and cries,
Knowing the winner would get a sweet prize.

Marty watched intently from his spot on the table,
Believing his new friend was willing and able.

There was a yelp of delight, then back in the boy ran
With Marty's butt clutched tightly in his little hand!

Marty was whole once again, relief flooded his face,
As he wrapped his rear end in a crunchy embrace.

The family said afikomen was part of dessert,
And Marty wasn't the slightest bit hurt.

All he'd ever wanted was to be a good meal,
So watching them nosh him was a pretty sweet deal.

They passed 'round his butt, Marty swelled with pride
To see Seder end with his delicious backside.

The End